Dedication from E. E. Arrendale

For Tommy

Dedication from Samantha Blessing Klotz

For my family, without whom I couldn't have done this work

Dedication from Rose Anne Stanard

For my family, whose loving support means everything

Blue Rooster Company
Publishing Coordinator - Gaëlle Freer www.bluerroosterco.org
Library of Congress Control Number: 2024903186
ISBN# 979-8-9899982-8-9 E.E. Arrendale

Twinkle
The Star Mouse

E. E. Arrendale
Illustration by Samantha Blessing Klotz
and Rose Anne Stanard

Twinkle the mouse loves the stars.
Every night he looks into the sky.
Twinkle watches the starlight and imagines
what creatures must live in the heavens.

"What are you doing, Twinkle?"
his mother asks.

"Wondering who lives in the stars,"
Twinkle replies.

"Come to dinner, baby, and eat all
your vegetables," she tells him.
"Maybe one day you will jump to the stars."
His brothers and sisters laugh.
But Twinkle eats his vegetables.

After dinner, Twinkle stands outside alone.
He jumps once but can't reach the stars.
He jumps twice, but still can't reach the stars.
Then, he closes his eyes,
stretches out his arms
and jumps with all his might.

About the Man in the Moon:

Darkened areas on the surface of the moon create the face of the Man-in-the-Moon. This coloration is created by meteorites hitting the moon. Ancient astronomers believed these dark areas were bodies of water and named them after seas and oceans.

Twinkle lands on the Moon.
There is a man in the Moon.
The Man-in-the-Moon has a round head.

"What are you doing here, little mouse?" The Man asks.

"I'd like to know who lives in the stars," says Twinkle.

"Jump there next." The Man looks up.
"Because tea is about to be served."

So, Twinkle jumps.

About the Seven Sisters

The cluster of stars called the Seven Sisters is properly known as the Pleiades. These stars were named for seven sisters who the Greek god Zeus turned into stars to hide from an overly eager Orion. Only six stars are visible today with the unaided eye.

The little mouse lands in a tea party.
There are Seven Sisters having tea and biscuits.

"Would you like some tea?" the Sisters ask.

"Thank you, I would," says Twinkle.
"I did not know
Seven Sisters live in the stars."

"Yes," they all say. "We live close together
so we may have tea parties."

After tea, Twinkle says, "thank you"
and jumps again.

About the Big Dipper and the Little Dipper:

Many cultures have seen these stars as different objects. They often are referred to as the Big Bear and the Little Bear, but the dippers have also been seen as a plow and a wagon.

He lands on a Big Dipper.
Twinkle slides down the handle and
falls into the Dipper. The Dipper
is full of warm milk.

Laughing, he climbs out
onto the handle of a Little Dipper.
But Twinkle is wet.
He slips.

This time, he falls
through the stars.

About Pegasus:

In Greek mythology the winged horse Pegasus flew so high he joined the gods in the stars. Many myths surround Pegasus, who was ridden by the Greek heroes Perseus and Bellerophon.

A flying horse saves Twinkle.

"I am Pegasus," the horse tells him.
"It is nice to meet you, little mouse."

Twinkle smiles. "Thank you,
Mr. Pegasus. I am trying to
see who lives in the stars."

"Then you should go here next.
You can help my friend."

Pegasus puts Twinkle near
a big star.

About Taurus:

The constellation Taurus is one of the most ancient symbols of the night sky. From the Sumerians to the Egyptians to the Greeks, many cultures could see the horns of a bull in the stars.

A huge bull comes next to Twinkle.
The bull snorts and stomps its hoof.

Twinkle is frightened.

But the bull softly nudges Twinkle,
turning over his hoof.
Twinkle takes a little star
out of the bull's hoof.

"That is much better," the bull smiles.
"I am Taurus. I stepped on
that falling star.
Pegasus said you wanted
to meet everyone.

Keep jumping, little mouse."
Twinkle jumps on.

About Scorpio:

The stars in the Scorpius constellation form a hook at the end of the pattern, which is the scorpion's stinger. The bright red star Antares, in the middle of the constellation, is the scorpion's heart.

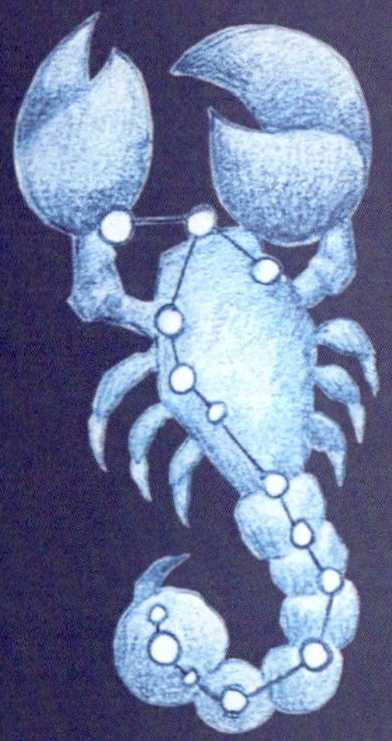

He lands on a scorpion.
The scorpion is very mad.

Twinkle runs away.
The scorpion chases him
and tries to sting him.
So Twinkle runs faster.

Then an arrow flies through
the stars next to the scorpion.

A giant hunter, with a bow and arrows,
stands next to Twinkle.

The scorpion runs away.

About Orion:

Named for a great hunter in Greco-Roman myths, the three stars of Orion's belt are some of the most easily recognizable stars in the night sky. According to legend, Orion and Scorpio are enemies.

"I am Orion," the hunter tells him.
"Scorpio is not all bad, but he has a nasty temper.
You must be careful, little mouse."

"Yes, sir, Mr. Orion," Twinkle says.
"But I am having fun in the stars."

"Indeed, Twinkle, but now you must do me a favor.
The heroes of the stars need the help
of someone very small and brave.

Jump to the next group of stars
where the heroes are planning."

About Hercules:

Considered the greatest hero in Greek mythology, Hercules was the son of Zeus, father of the gods, and a mortal woman. To celebrate his great achievements, the gods placed his likeness in the stars.

Twinkle lands and sees two heroes.
One wears a lion skin and carries a giant club.
The other has a sword and a helmet.

"Hello," says Twinkle shyly. "I am Twinkle
and Mr. Orion sent me to help."

"We are glad you have come,"
says the hero with the club.

"I am Hercules, and this is
my friend Perseus.
We have a problem.

Are you brave, little mouse?"

Twinkle nods 'yes.'

About Draco:

Ancient peoples have seen a dragon in this group of winding stars. For the Greeks, Draco represents a dragon hurled into the stars by the goddess Athena during a battle between the Greek Gods and the Titans.

"We have been in a battle!
Draco the Dragon and
Cancer the Crab kidnapped
the princess Andromeda," Perseus says.

"This is very sad. All the stars must
move across the night sky.
If Andromeda isn't here to do this –
the sun will not rise!"

Mighty Hercules looks at Twinkle.
"When we try to rescue the princess,
Draco comes to fight us.
But just as we are about to win,
Cancer moves the princess
and Draco runs away."

About Perseus:

In mythology Perseus rescued the princess Andromeda from a great sea monster – the Kraken (Cetus). In August, the Perseid meteor showers are visible in the Perseus constellation.

Twinkle thinks hard.

"Do you need me to sneak past Cancer and rescue the princess?" Twinkle asks.

The heroes agree. It is just what they need.

"I will do my best," says Twinkle.

Hercules and Perseus
go to fight the dragon.
Draco is scary and the battle
makes terrible noises.

Twinkle sneaks carefully around
the great fighters.

About Cancer:

In ancient times, the sun would reach its most northern point in the sky in the constellation Cancer (Tropic of Cancer) and then move backwards (like a crab) to the south. Cancer and Hercules are enemies in Greek mythology.

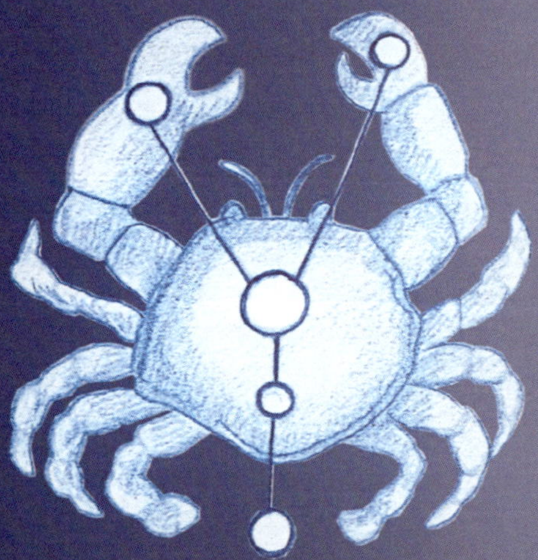

Twinkle sees Cancer the Crab.
The crab has giant claws and
does not look nice.

Twinkle isn't sure he's brave anymore.

But Cancer does not see him,
and Twinkle remembers his promise.

Slowly, slowly he goes under the crab.
Twinkle sees a beautiful princess
tied to a rock.

About the Stars:

Our universe is always changing and expanding, but these shifts may only be observed over long periods. The stars appear to be 'moving' in the night sky because of the spinning earth. The earth's rotation 'moves' the stars from east to west every night.

Twinkle scampers up the rock
and chews away at the ropes.

Andromeda smiles at the little mouse.

As soon as the ropes break,
she puts Twinkle in her pocket
and runs away.

The heroes see the princess escape
and stop the fight.

Draco and Cancer are very angry.

But it is too late.

About Andromeda:

Sometimes known as the chained maiden, Andromeda was bound to a rock by her parents, Cepheus and Cassiopeia, as a sacrifice to the sea monster Cetus. Perseus rescued her.

"Thank you, my three heroes,"
Andromeda says.

"You are very brave
for such a tiny mouse.

Now I must move across the sky
so the sun will rise.

You should jump home now
but come back soon,"
Andromeda tells him.

Twinkle waves 'good-bye'
and jumps home.

Twinkle's mother finds him asleep.
She caresses him.

"Mother," says sleepy Twinkle.
"I jumped to the stars and had tea
with Seven Sisters, fell in the Big Dipper,
rode on Pegasus, helped Taurus, ran from Scorpio,
was saved by Orion, and sneaked past Draco and
Cancer to rescue the princess Andromeda
with Hercules and Perseus.
It was wonderful."

Twinkle takes a deep breath
and rests his head.

His mother kisses his cheek and smiles.
"So that is who lives in the stars," she thinks.

THE END

Teacher Notes and Resources:

Thoughts and ideas for teaching astronomy.
Draw a distinction between astonomy, the study of the stars and planets and astology, the understanding that the stars and planets affect our lives and actions.

Consider a field trip to a planetarium

Ancient use of sun and stars:
Study of Stonehenge, the Egyptian pyramids, the Aztec pyramids and their correlation with astronomical phenomena.

Telescope lesson:
Discuss how a telescope works. Learn the various sizes of telescopes. Understand how the size affects what you can see.

Learn how to find constellations in the night sky. Learn how seasons affect planet and star positions. Learn stories behind the names of the dark and light areas of the moon's surface.

Discuss the history of how constellations have been used for navigation by sailors and other travelers.

Art Projects:
Build a 3 dimensional model or cut out paper representation of sun and planets. Add the constellations in a background panel.

Dramatic presentation ideas:
Act out the challenge between Hercules and Orion with Draco.

Use the book as a script with different students for each part. Learn about the stars in the constellations as Greek heroes and villains.

Other interactive projects to enrich the student experience:

Read about Greek and Roman mythology. Learn about the two different naming systems and where they overlap.

View Disney's animated "Hercules." Watch for constellations shown in the story.

Learn about Pegasus and horses in history. How would a horse with wings take off and fly?

Additional Resources for Constellations:

Resource for educators: **discoverspace.org**

For educators: **nasa.gov**

K-12 Space STEM Resources/Smithsonian Science Education Center: **ssec.si.edu**

Educator Resources/Space & Rocket Center: **rocketcenter.com**

United Kingdom Archives -National Geographic for Kids: **natgeokids.com**

Teaching Activities About Space: **sciencejournalforkids.org**

About the Illustrations in This Book:

Each illustration was drawn with non-waxy colored pencils. The background constellations were created with Japanese inks, chalk pastels and watercolor paints on premium watercolor paper. The final art was produced by combining the constellations and pencil drawings in Adobe Photoshop®.

Twinkle
The Star Mouse
(coloring page)